THE WORDS OF

MARTIN LUTHER KING, JR.

———

Presented By Mayor Andrew Young

On The Occasion Of The

Democratic National Convention

July 18–21, 1988

Atlanta, Georgia

———

THE WORDS OF
MARTIN LUTHER KING, JR.

SELECTED BY
CORETTA SCOTT KING

Newmarket Press
New York

Library of Congress Cataloging in Publication Data

King, Martin Luther.
   The words of Martin Luther King, Jr.

   Bibliography: p.
   1. King, Martin Luther—Quotations.   2. Afro-Americans
—Civil rights—Quotations, maxims, etc.   3. United
States—Race relations—Quotations, maxims, etc.
I. King, Coretta Scott, 1927–   II. Title.
E185.97.K5A25   1984   323.4'092'4   83-17306
ISBN 0-937858-28-5 (Hardcover)
ISBN 0-937858-79-X (Paperback)
Design by Ruth Kolbert, based on a design for *The Words of Gandhi* by Leslie Miller for Byron Preiss Visual Publications, Inc.

To the unsung heroes and heroines of the Nonviolent Civil Rights Movement whose commitment, courage, dedication and determination to achieve freedom, justice and equality, inspired Martin Luther King, Jr., to create the beautiful prose which is inscribed across these pages

CONTENTS

INTRODUCTION
by Coretta Scott King

My husband, Martin Luther King, Jr., was a man who had hoped
to be a Baptist preacher to a large, Southern, urban congregation.
Instead, by the time he died in 1968, he had led millions of people
into shattering forever the Southern system of segregation of the
races. He had fashioned a mass black electorate that eliminated
overt racism from political campaigns and accumulated political
power for blacks beyond any they had ever possessed in the United
States. Above all, he brought a new and higher dimension of
human dignity to black people's lives.

I met Martin in Boston in 1952, when he was twenty-three
years old. I had grown up in rural Alabama, attended Antioch
College in Ohio, and was studying music at the New England
Conservatory. Martin was working toward a doctor of philosophy
degree at Boston University. Before coming to Boston, Martin had
earned a B.A. in sociology from Morehouse College in Atlanta
and a B.D. from Crozer Theological Seminary in Pennsylvania.
His father, Reverend Martin Luther King, Sr., a sharecropper's
son, was pastor of the Ebenezer Baptist Church in Atlanta. His
mother, Alberta Williams King, was a minister's daughter. Martin
felt a deeply serious call to the ministry when he was a seventeen-
year-old junior at Morehouse. At the age of eighteen he was
ordained and made an assistant pastor at Ebenezer Church. I
thought I did not want to marry a minister, but Martin was an
unusual person. He was such a good man. If he ever did something
a little wrong, or committed a selfish act, his conscience devoured
him. At the same time he was so alive and so much fun to be with.
He had a strength that he imparted to me and others that he met.

Martin always had a deep commitment to helping his fellow
human beings. He told me that the turning point in his thinking
about how to reconcile Christian pacifism with getting things done
came while he was at the seminary, when he learned about the
revered Indian leader, Mahatma Gandhi. Martin later wrote in

Stride Toward Freedom: "Gandhi was probably the first person in history to lift the love ethic of Jesus above mere interaction between individuals to a powerful and effective social force on a large scale.... It was in this Gandhian emphasis on love and non-violence that I discovered the method for social reform that I had been seeking for so many months."

Martin and I were married in 1953. The next year, Martin took up his first pastorate, at the Dexter Avenue Church in Montgomery, Alabama. We moved back to the South, which was still the totally segregated society into which we had been born. In 1954 the United States Supreme Court ruled that separate educational facilities for black and white children were unequal and unconstitutional. Further court decisions requiring school integration produced violent reactions in the South. White Citizens Councils sprang up in attempts to nullify the court's decisions, and the Ku Klux Klan got out its sheets and hoods and paraded and set crosses on fire. All public facilities continued to be forcibly segregated. High taxes at the voting polling places prevented most blacks from being able to cast their ballots.

In Montgomery, some of the most degrading facets of segregation were the rules of the Montgomery City Bus Lines. Blacks were required to sit and stand at the rear of the buses, even if there were empty seats in the front section, which was reserved for whites. Furthermore, blacks had to pay their fares at the front of the bus, get off and walk to the rear to reboard through the back door. Drivers often pulled off and left them after they had paid their fares. On December 1, 1955, Mrs. Rosa Parks, a woman highly respected in the black community, boarded a bus to return home after her day's work as a seamstress in a downtown department store. She sat down in the first row behind the section reserved for whites. Soon the bus driver ordered Mrs. Parks to give up her seat to a boarding white man and stand farther back in the bus. When she quietly and tiredly refused, the driver got off the bus to get a policeman, who arrested her. At the courthouse, Mrs. Parks called her friend E. D. Nixon, who came down and signed a bail bond for her. Mr. Nixon phoned Martin and me the next day to describe the incident and to urge a boycott of the buses. "It's the only way to make the white folks see that we will not take this sort of thing any longer," he said.

Martin agreed and offered the Dexter Avenue Baptist Church as a meeting place. Over forty leaders from all segments of the black community came to the meeting. They formed the Montgomery Improvement Association (MIA), elected Martin president, and organized a boycott starting on December 5. For over a year, the fifty thousand black people in Montgomery walked and car-pooled to their jobs, schools, and churches. The white city leadership decided to find excuses to arrest blacks when they saw that the boycott was really working. One day, after picking up three passengers at a parking lot car-pool station, Martin was followed by a motorcycle cop. He obeyed all the traffic rules scrupulously, but when he let off his passengers the cop ordered him out of his car and arrested him for going 30 miles per hour in a 25-mile-per-hour zone. At the city jail he was thrown into a segregated, dingy cell with other black protestors. News of Martin's arrest spread quickly, and after many blacks gathered outside the jail, he was fingerprinted and released on his own recognizance.

We began getting death threats and abusive phone calls. One night, while Martin was at an MIA mass rally, I was at home with a friend and our first child, two-month-old Yolanda, when a bomb hit our front porch and exploded. Alerted by the threats, we had rushed to the back of the house instead of the front when we heard the thud of the bomb, and fortunately no one was hurt.

Such arrests and acts of violence only consolidated the boycotters and raised enthusiasm for our nonviolent protest movement. We realized the movement was more than local; it was a surge toward a national, even international, assertion of the individual's right to freedom and self-respect. It led to the Supreme Court's affirmation that Alabama's laws requiring segregation on buses were unconstitutional. On December 21, 1956, Montgomery's buses were peacefully integrated.

As I wrote later in my book, *My Life with Martin Luther King, Jr.,* "Montgomery was the soil in which the seed of a new theory of social action took root. Black people had found in non-violent direct action a militant method that avoided violence but achieved dramatic confrontation, which electrified and educated the whole nation.... Without hatred or abjectly bending their knees, the demand for freedom emerged in strength and dignity. Black people had been waiting for this, and instinctively they seized the new method and opened a new era of social change."

Martin was now a hero to America's black people. Shortly after the boycott, *Time* magazine ran a cover story on Martin, calling him "the scholarly Negro Baptist minister who in little more than a year has risen from nowhere to become one of the nation's remarkable leaders of men."

Inspired by the Montgomery bus victory, movements sprang up in other cities. Martin thought all these activities should be coordinated to have the broadest good effect. After a series of meetings, the first of which was held at the Ebenezer Baptist Church in Atlanta, we helped found the Southern Christian Leadership Conference (SCLC) in 1957. Martin was elected president. From the first, the SCLC was church oriented in leadership and membership and in the concept of nonviolence. Martin did not call for disobedience of all laws, only for disobedience of unjust laws. He always believed in the supremacy of a higher moral law.

Between 1957 and 1959, Martin commuted between Montgomery and SCLC headquarters in Atlanta. He was invited to preach and lecture throughout the country. We visited Ghana in 1957, attending that nation's independence celebration as guests of Kwame Nkrumah, and in 1959 went on a pilgrimage to India to better understand Gandhi's nonviolent philosophy; there we were received by Prime Minister Nehru. Toward the end of 1959, Martin realized he had to devote full time and effort to the civil rights struggle, and so in 1960 we left our wonderful Dexter congregation and moved to Atlanta, where Martin became copastor with his father of the Ebenezer Baptist Church.

Demonstrations were continuing throughout the South with some successes. There were sit-ins to desegregate lunch counters and restaurants. The first group of Freedom Riders, black and white people organized by the Congress for Racial Equality to protest segregation on interstate buses, left Washington, D.C., by Greyhound on May 4, 1961. SCLC backed the Freedom Rides, and Martin served as chairman of their coordinating committee. Ten days later the first bus was burned outside of Anniston, Alabama. A white mob beat the Riders when they arrived in Birmingham. They were arrested in Jackson, Mississippi, and spent two months in Parchman Penitentiary. But the Freedom Rides continued.

In Birmingham, one of the most segregated cities in the country, George Wallace pledged at his inauguration as governor, "Segregation now, segregation tomorrow, segregation forever!" Eugene ("Bull") Connor was Birmingham's Director of Public Safety and relied on brute force against Negroes and peaceful demonstrators. He ordered the use of police dogs and fire hoses against children who were marching in a peaceful protest.

SCLC decided to join the Alabama Christian Movement for Human Rights in a massive campaign against segregation in Birmingham. Protests started in April 1963, with lunch-counter sit-ins. After city officials obtained an Alabama state court injunction against the demonstrators, Martin and other leaders determined to defy the injunction. On Good Friday they set off from church, marching peacefully. Bull Connor ordered them all arrested. Martin used the time in prison to write his now-famous "Letter from Birmingham Jail," in which he explained to a group of white clergymen publicly critical of his activities the necessity for peaceful protest to bring about social change.

While Martin was held incommunicado in jail, President John Kennedy and Attorney General Robert Kennedy helped me find out what was going on. They directed public attention to the Birmingham situation, which finally culminated in a real victory for the movement when white city officials and merchants sat down with black leaders to hammer out a settlement. Peaceful integration came because militant nonviolence forced negotiation and agreement.

After Birmingham, nearly a thousand cities became engulfed in protests against segregation. This encouraged us to join in organizing a march on Washington to dramatize the need for new federal legislation to integrate blacks completely into American society. On August 28, 1963, we participated in a mass rally with 250,000 people who had traveled from all over the country to Washington, D.C. Martin delivered his "I Have A Dream" speech from the steps of the Lincoln Memorial, and afterward President Kennedy met with the leaders of the march. Martin wrote about that day in *Why We Can't Wait:* "As television beamed the image of this extraordinary gathering across the border oceans, everyone who believed in man's capacity to better himself had a moment of inspiration and confidence in the future of the human race. And every dedicated American could be proud that a dynamic experience of democracy in his nation's capital has been made visible to the world."

In October 1964, we learned that Martin had been awarded the Nobel Peace Prize. He and I were overcome with pride and joy and a tremendous feeling of responsibility. This was not just a prize for civil rights but for contributing to world peace. Martin said in his acceptance speech in Oslo, "I feel as though this prize has been given to me for something that really has *not* yet been achieved. It is a commission to go out and work even harder for the things in which we believe." Martin divided the $54,000 prize among SCLC, Congress of Racial Equality, Student Nonviolent Coordinating Committee, NAACP, National Council of Negro Women, and the American Foundation on Nonviolence.

By the summer of 1965, President Johnson, with the support of the civil rights community and its allies, had pushed through Congress and signed into law the long-awaited Civil Rights and Voting Rights acts, which finally put the federal government behind integration. But many of the urban ghettos in the North were erupting in violence. Many Americans were also disturbed by their country's drawn-out involvement in the Vietnam war. In 1965 Martin made a statement: "I'm not going to sit by and see war escalated without saying anything about it. It is worthless to talk about integration if there is no world to integrate. The war in Vietnam must be stopped." In 1966 he agreed to serve as cochairman of Clergy and Laymen Concerned About Vietnam.

In 1968 Martin was deeply involved in organizing a Poor People's Campaign to demonstrate in a mass way for economic as well as civil rights, which he had always considered dependent upon each other. He went to Memphis, Tennessee, to lead six thousand protestors on a march in support of striking sanitation workers. On April 4, while Martin stood talking on the second-floor balcony of his Memphis motel room, a sniper shot and killed him. He was thirty-nine years old.

During his lifetime, Martin wrote three books and saw his speeches and sermons collected in two additional volumes. I hope that this collection of quotations, drawn from these works as well as from other speeches and articles, will remind readers what Martin Luther King, Jr., lived and stood for and how much remains for all of us to do today. Martin always pleaded for positive, constructive action. The triple evils of poverty, racism, and war were his concerns wherever they were found in the world. He devoted his life to the process of uprooting them. By reaching into and beyond ourselves and tapping the transcendent ethic of love, we shall overcome these evils. Love, truth, and the courage to do what is right should be our own guideposts on this lifelong journey.

THE
COMMUNITY
OF MAN

"An individual has not started living until he can rise above the narrow confines of his individualistic concerns to the broader concerns of all humanity."

"Every man must decide whether he will walk in the light of creative altruism or the darkness of destructive selfishness. This is the judgment. Life's most persistent and urgent question is, What are you doing for others?"

"Everybody can be great. Because anybody can serve. You don't have to have a college degree to serve. You don't have to make your subject and your verb agree to serve. You don't have to know about Plato and Aristotle to serve. You don't have to know Einstein's theory of relativity to serve. You don't have to know the second theory of thermo-dynamics in physics to serve. You only need a heart full of grace. A soul generated by love."

"Love is the only force capable of transforming an enemy into a friend."

"All men are interdependent. Every nation is an heir of a vast treasury of ideas and labor to which both the living and the dead of all nations have contributed. Whether we realize it or not, each of us lives eternally 'in the red.' We are everlasting debtors to known and unknown men and women. When we arise in the morning, we go into the bathroom where we reach for a sponge which is provided for us by a Pacific islander. We reach for soap that is created for us by a European. Then at the table we drink coffee which is provided for us by a South American, or tea by a Chinese, or cocoa by a West African. Before we leave for our jobs we are already beholden to more than half of the world."

"All too many of those who live in affluent America ignore those who exist in poor America; in doing so, the affluent Americans will eventually have to face themselves with the question that Eichmann chose to ignore: How responsible am I for the well-being of my fellows? To ignore evil is to become an accomplice to it."

"It is still one of the tragedies of human history that the 'children of darkness' are frequently more determined and zealous than the 'children of light.' "

"Mammoth productive facilities with computer minds, cities that engulf the landscape and pierce the clouds, planes that almost outrace time—these are awesome, but they cannot be spiritually inspiring. Nothing in our glittering technology can raise man to new heights, because material growth has been made an end in itself, and, in the absence of moral purpose, man himself becomes smaller as the works of man become bigger. Gargantuan industry and government, woven into an intricate computerized mechanism, leave the person outside. The sense of participation is lost, the feeling that ordinary individuals influence important decisions vanishes, and man becomes separated and diminished.

"When an individual is no longer a true participant, when he no longer feels a sense of responsibility to his society, the content of democracy is emptied. When culture is degraded and vulgarity enthroned, when the social system does not build security but induces peril, inexorably the individual is impelled to pull away from a soulless society. This process produces alienation—perhaps the most pervasive and insidious development in contemporary society."

"Moral principles have lost their distinctiveness. For modern man, absolute right and absolute wrong are a matter of what the majority is doing. Right and wrong are relative to likes and dislikes and the customs of a particular community. We have unconsciously applied Einstein's theory of relativity, which properly described the physical universe, to the moral and ethical realm."

"We are prone to judge success by the index of our salaries or the size of our automobiles, rather than by the quality of our service and relationship to humanity."

"As long as there is poverty in the world I can never be rich, even if I have a billion dollars. As long as diseases are rampant and millions of people in this world cannot expect to live more than twenty-eight or thirty years, I can never be totally healthy even if I just got a good checkup at Mayo Clinic. I can never be what I ought to be until you are what you ought to be. This is the way our world is made. No individual or nation can stand out boasting of being independent. We are interdependent."

"In a multiracial society no group can make it alone. It is a myth to believe that the Irish, the Italians, and the Jews . . . rose to power through separatism. It is true that they stuck together. But their group unity was always enlarged by joining in alliances with other groups such as political machines and trade unions. To succeed in a pluralistic society, and an often hostile one at that, the Negro obviously needs organized strength, but that strength will only be effective when it is consolidated through constructive alliances with the majority group."

"In the final analysis the white man cannot ignore the Negro's problem, because he is a part of the Negro and the Negro is a part of him. The Negro's agony diminishes the white man, and the Negro's salvation enlarges the white man.

"What is needed today on the part of white America is a committed altruism which recognizes this truth. True altruism is more than the capacity to pity; it is the capacity to empathize. Pity is feeling sorry for someone; empathy is feeling sorry with someone. Empathy is fellow feeling for the person in need—his pain, agony, and burdens. I doubt if the problems of our teeming ghettos will have a great chance to be solved until the white majority, through genuine empathy, comes to feel the ache and anguish of the Negroes' daily life."

"Our cultural patterns are an amalgam of black and white. Our destinies are tied together. There is no separate black path to power and fulfillment that does not have to intersect with white roots. Somewhere along the way the two must join together, black and white together, we shall overcome, and I still believe it."

"We must develop and maintain the capacity to forgive. He who is devoid of the power to forgive is devoid of the power to love. There is some good in the worst of us and some evil in the best of us. When we discover this, we are less prone to hate our enemies."

"Forgiveness is not an occasional act; it is a permanent attitude."

"A man who won't die for something is not fit to live."

"The ultimate measure of a man is not where he stands in moments of comfort and convenience, but where he stands at times of challenge and controversy. The true neighbor will risk his position, his prestige, and even his life for the welfare of others. In dangerous valleys and hazardous pathways, he will lift some bruised and beaten brother to a higher and more noble life."

"Courage faces fear and thereby masters it. Cowardice represses fear and is thereby mastered by it. Courageous men never lose the zest for living even though their life situation is zestless; cowardly men, overwhelmed by the uncertainties of life, lose the will to live. We must constantly build dykes of courage to hold back the flood of fear."

"Many people fear nothing more terribly than to take a position which stands out sharply and clearly from the prevailing opinion. The tendency of most is to adopt a view that is so ambiguous that it will include everything and so popular that it will include everybody. Not a few men who cherish lofty and noble ideals hide them under a bushel for fear of being called different."

"We must accept finite disappointment, but we must never lose infinite hope."

"I have the audacity to believe that peoples everywhere can have three meals a day for their bodies, education and culture for their minds, and dignity, equality, and freedom for their spirits. I believe that what self-centered men have torn down, other-centered men can build up."

RACISM

"Every parent at some time faces the problem of explaining the facts of life to his child. Just as inevitably, for the Negro parent, the moment comes when he must explain to his offspring the facts of segregation. My mother took me on her lap and began by telling me about slavery and how it had ended with the Civil War. She tried to explain the divided system of the South—the segregated schools, restaurants, theaters, housing; the white and colored signs on drinking fountains, waiting rooms, lavatories—as a social condition rather than a natural order. Then she said the words that almost every Negro hears before he can yet understand the injustice that makes them necessary: 'You are as good as anyone.'"

"My mother, as the daughter of a successful minister, had grown up in comparative comfort. She had been sent to the best available school and college and had, in general, been protected from the worst blights of discrimination. But my father, a sharecropper's son, had met its brutalities at first hand, and had begun to strike back at an early age.

"I remembered riding with him [one day in my childhood] when he accidentally drove past a stop sign. A policeman pulled up to the car and said, 'All right, boy, pull over and let me see your license.'

"My father replied indignantly, 'I'm no boy.' Then, pointing to me, 'This is a boy. I'm a man, and until you call me one, I will not listen to you.'

"The policeman was so shocked that he wrote the ticket up nervously and left the scene as quickly as possible.

"With this heritage, it is not surprising that I had . . . learned to abhor segregation, considering it both rationally inexplicable and morally unjustifiable."

"The straitjackets of race prejudice and discrimination do not wear only Southern labels. The subtle, psychological technique of the North has approached in its ugliness and victimization of the Negro the outright terror and open brutality of the South."

"There is little hope for us until we become tough-minded enough to break loose from the shackles of prejudice, half-truths, and downright ignorance."

"Being a Negro in America is not a comfortable existence. It means being a part of the company of the bruised, the battered, the scarred, and the defeated. Being a Negro in America means trying to smile when you want to cry. It means trying to hold on to physical life amid psychological death. It means the pain of watching your children grow up with clouds of inferiority in their mental skies. It means having your legs cut off, and then being condemned for being a cripple. It means seeing your mother and father spiritually murdered by the slings and arrows of daily exploitation, and then being hated for being an orphan. Being a Negro in America means listening to suburban politicians talk eloquently against open housing while arguing in the same breath that they are not racists. It means being harried by day and haunted by night by a nagging sense of nobodiness and constantly fighting to be saved from the poison of bitterness. It means the ache and anguish of living in so many situations where hopes unborn have died."

"The daily life of the Negro is still lived in the basement of the Great Society. He is still at the bottom despite the few who have penetrated to slightly higher levels. Even where the door has been forced partially open, mobility for the Negro is still sharply restricted. There is often no bottom at which to start, and when there is, there is almost always no room at the top."

"To develop a sense of black consciousness and peoplehood does not require that we scorn the white race as a whole. It is not the race per se that we fight but the policies and ideology that leaders of that race have formulated to perpetuate oppression."

"A doctrine of black supremacy is as evil as a doctrine of white supremacy."

"Like life, racial understanding is not something that we find but something that we must create. And so the ability of Negroes and whites to work together, to understand each other, will not be found readymade; it must be created by the fact of contact."

"We must use time creatively, in the knowledge that the time is always ripe to do right. Now is the time to make real the promise of democracy and transform our pending national elegy into a creative psalm of brotherhood. Now is the time to lift our national policy from the quicksand of racial injustice to the solid rock of human dignity."

CIVIL RIGHTS

"It is pretty difficult to like some people. Like is sentimental and it is pretty difficult to like someone bombing your home; it is pretty difficult to like somebody threatening your children; it is difficult to like congressmen who spend all of their time trying to defeat civil rights. But Jesus says love them, and love is greater than like."

"For years now we have heard the word 'Wait!' It rings in the ear of every Negro with piercing familiarity.

"Perhaps it is easy for those who have never felt the stinging darts of segregation to say, 'Wait.' But when you have seen vicious mobs lynch your mothers and fathers at will and drown your sisters and brothers at whim; when you have seen hate-filled policemen curse, kick, and even kill your black brothers and sisters; when you see the vast majority of your twenty million Negro brothers smothering in an airtight cage of poverty in the midst of an affluent society . . . when you are forever fighting a degenerating sense of 'nobodiness'—then you will understand why we find it difficult to wait."

"Nothing provides the communists with a better climate for expansion and infiltration than the continued alliance of our nation with racism and exploitation throughout the world. And if we are not diligent in our determination to root out the last vestiges of racism in our dealings with the rest of the world, we may soon see the sins of our fathers visited upon ours and succeeding generations. For the conditions which are so classically represented in Africa are present also in Asia and in our own backyard in Latin America."

"Oppressed people cannot remain oppressed forever. The yearning for freedom eventually manifests itself, and that is what has happened to the American Negro. Something within has reminded him of his birthright of freedom, and something without has reminded him that it can be gained. Consciously or unconsciously, he has been caught up by the *Zeitgeist,* and with his black brothers of Africa and his brown and yellow brothers of Asia, South America, and the Caribbean, the United States Negro is moving with a sense of great urgency toward the promised land of racial justice."

"It is one thing to agree that the goal of integration is morally and legally right; it is another thing to commit oneself positively and actively to the ideal of integration— the former is intellectual assent, the latter is actual belief. These are days that demand practices to match professions. This is no day to pay lip service to integration, we must pay *life* service to it."

"Through education we seek to change attitudes; through legislation and court orders we seek to regulate behavior. Through education we seek to change internal feelings (prejudice, hate, etc.); through legislation and court orders we seek to control the external effects of those feelings. Through education we seek to break down the spiritual barriers to integration; through legislation and court orders we seek to break down the physical barriers to integration. One method is not a substitute for the other, but a meaningful and necessary supplement. Anyone who starts out with the conviction that the road to racial justice is only one lane wide will inevitably create a traffic jam and make the journey infinitely longer."

"I often wonder whether or not education is fulfilling its purpose. A great majority of the so-called education people do not think logically and scientifically. Even the press, the classroom, the platform, and the pulpit in many instances do not give us objective and unbiased truths. To save man from the morass of propaganda, in my opinion, is one of the chief aims of education. Education must enable one to sift and weigh evidence, to discern the true from the false, the real from the unreal, and the facts from fiction.

"The function of education, therefore, is to teach one to think intensively and to think critically. But education which stops with efficiency may prove the greatest menace to society. The most dangerous criminal may be the man gifted with reason but with no morals.

"We must remember that intelligence is not enough. Intelligence plus character—that is the goal of true education. The complete education gives one not only power of concentration but worthy objectives upon which to concentrate. The broad education will, therefore, transmit to one not only the accumulated knowledge of the race but also the accumulated experience of social living."

"Morals cannot be legislated, but behavior can be regulated. The law cannot make an employer love me, but it can keep him from refusing to hire me because of the color of my skin."

"There comes a time when a moral man can't obey a law which his conscience tells him is unjust. And the important thing is that when he does that, he willingly accepts the penalty—because if he refuses to accept the penalty, then he becomes reckless, and he becomes an anarchist. There were those individuals in every age and generation who were willing to say, 'I will be obedient to a higher law.' It is important to see that there are times when a manmade law is out of harmony with the moral law of the universe."

"There is nothing that expressed massive civil disobedience any more than the Boston Tea Party, and yet we give this to our young people and our students as a part of the great tradition of our nation. So I think we are in good company when we break unjust laws, and I think those who are willing to do it and accept the penalty are those who are part of the saving of the nation."

"Our nettlesome task is to discover how to organize our strength into compelling power so that government cannot elude our demands. We must develop, from strength, a situation in which the government finds it wise and prudent to collaborate with us. It would be the height of naïveté to wait passively until the administration had somehow been infused with such blessings of good will that it implored us for our programs. The first course is grounded in mature realism; the other is childish fantasy."

"The Negro cannot win . . . if he is willing to sell the future of his children for his personal and immediate comfort and safety."

"We can never be satisfied as long as a Negro in Mississippi cannot vote and a Negro in New York believes he has nothing for which to vote."

"Many white Americans of good will have never connected bigotry with economic exploitation. They have deplored prejudice but tolerated or ignored economic injustice. But the Negro knows that these two evils have a malignant kinship."

"New laws are not enough. The emergency we now face is economic, and it is a desperate and worsening situation. For the 35 million poor people in America . . . there is a kind of strangulation in the air. In our society it is murder, psychologically, to deprive a man of a job or an income. You are in substance saying to that man that he has no right to exist."

"This is no time to engage in the luxury of cooling off or to take the tranquilizing drug of gradualism. Now is the time to make real the promises of democracy."

"It is impossible to create a formula for the future which does not take into account that our society has been doing something special *against* the Negro for hundreds of years. How then can he be absorbed into the mainstream of American life if we do not do something special *for* him now, in order to balance the equation and equip him to compete on a just and equal basis?

"What will it profit him to be able to send his children to an integrated school if the family income is insufficient to buy them school clothes? What will he gain by being permitted to move to an integrated neighborhood if he cannot afford to do so because he is unemployed or has a low-paying job with no future?

"In asking for something special, the Negro is not seeking charity. He does not want to languish on welfare rolls any more than the next man. He does not want to be given a job he cannot handle. Neither, however, does he want to be told that there is no place where he can be trained to handle it.

"Few people consider the fact that, in addition to being enslaved for two centuries, the Negro was, during all those years, robbed of the wages of his toil. No amount of gold could provide an adequate compensation for the exploitation and humiliation of the Negro in America down through the centuries. Not all the wealth of this affluent society could meet the bill. Yet a price can be placed on unpaid wages."

"The Negro freedom movement would have been historic and worthy even if it had only served the cause of civil rights. But its laurels are greater because it stimulated a broader social movement that elevated the moral level of the nation. In the struggle against the preponderant evils of the society, decent values were preserved. Moreover, a significant body of young people learned that in opposing the tyrannical forces that were crushing them they added stature and meaning to their lives. The Negro and white youth who in alliance fought bruising engagements with the status quo inspired each other with a sense of moral mission, and both gave the nation an example of self-sacrifice and dedication."

"I think the greatest victory of this period was . . . something internal. The real victory was what this period did to the psyche of the black man. The greatness of this period was that we armed ourselves with dignity and self-respect. The greatness of this period was that we straightened our backs up. And a man can't ride your back unless it's bent."

JUSTICE
AND
FREEDOM

"Words cannot express the exultation felt by the individual as he finds himself, with hundreds of his fellows, behind prison bars for a cause he knows is just."

"Freedom is never voluntarily given by the oppressor; it must be demanded by the oppressed."

"Freedom has always been an expensive thing. History is fit testimony to the fact that freedom is rarely gained without sacrifice and self-denial."

"When evil men plot, good men must plan. When evil men burn and bomb, good men must build and bind. When evil men shout ugly words of hatred, good men must commit themselves to the glories of love. Where evil men would seek to perpetuate an unjust status quo, good men must seek to bring into being a real order of justice."

"It is time that we stopped our blithe lip service to the guarantees of life, liberty, and pursuit of happiness. These fine sentiments are embodied in the Declaration of Independence, but that document was always a declaration of intent rather than of reality. There were slaves when it was written; there were still slaves when it was adopted; and to this day, black Americans have not life, liberty, nor the privilege of pursuing happiness, and millions of poor white Americans are in economic bondage that is scarcely less oppressive. Americans who genuinely treasure our national ideals, who know they are still elusive dreams for all too many, should welcome the stirring of Negro demands. They are shattering the complacency that allowed a multitude of social evils to accumulate. Negro agitation is requiring America to reexamine its comforting myths and may yet catalyze the drastic reforms that will save us from social catastrophe."

"There comes a time when people get tired of being trampled by oppression. There comes a time when people get tired of being plunged into the abyss of exploitation and nagging injustice. The story of Montgomery is the story of fifty thousand such Negroes who were willing to substitute tired feet for tired souls, and walk the streets of Montgomery until the walls of segregation were finally battered by the forces of justice."

"Our freedom was not won a century ago, it is not won today; but some small part of it is in our hands, and we are marching no longer by ones and twos but in legions of thousands, convinced now it cannot be denied by any human force.

"Today the question is not whether we shall be free but by what course we will win. In the recent past our struggle has had two phases. The first phase began in the early 1950s when Negroes slammed the door shut on submission and subservience. Adapting nonviolent resistance to conditions in the United States, we swept into Southern streets to demand our citizenship and manhood. For the South, with its complex system of brutal segregation, we were inaugurating a rebellion. Merely to march in public streets was to rock the status quo to its roots. Boycotting buses in Montgomery; demonstrating in Birmingham, the citadel of segregation; and defying guns, dogs, and clubs in Selma, while maintaining disciplined nonviolence, totally confused the rulers of the South. If they let us march, they admitted their lie that the black man was content. If they shot us down, they told the world they were inhuman brutes."

"A child of no more than eight walked with her mother one day in a demonstration. An amused policeman leaned down to her and said with mock gruffness, 'What do you want?'

"The child looked into his eyes, unafraid, and gave her answer.

" 'F'eedom,' she said.

"She could not even pronounce the word, but no Gabriel trumpet could have sounded a truer note."

"A hundred times I have been asked why we have allowed little children to march in demonstrations, to freeze and suffer in jails, to be exposed to bullets and dynamite. The questions imply that we have revealed a want of family feeling or a recklessness toward family security. The answer is simple. Our children and our families are maimed a little every day of our lives. If we can end an incessant torture by a single climactic confrontation, the risks are acceptable. Moreover, our family life will be born anew if we fight together. Other families may be fortunate enough to be able to protect their young from danger. Our families, as we have seen, are different. Oppression has again and again divided and splintered them. We are a people torn apart from era to era. It is logical, moral, and psychologically constructive for us to resist oppression united as families. Out of this unity, out of the bond of fighting together, forges will come. The inner strength and integrity will make us whole again."

"Let us say it boldly, that if the total slum violations of law by the white man over the years were calculated and were compared with the lawbreaking of a few days of riots, the hardened criminal would be the white man."

"The majority of white Americans consider themselves sincerely committed to justice for the Negro. They believe that American society is essentially hospitable to fair play and to steady growth toward a middle-class Utopia embodying racial harmony. But unfortunately this is a fantasy of self-deception and comfortable vanity. Overwhelmingly America is still struggling with irresolution and contradictions. It has been sincere and even ardent in welcoming some change. But too quickly apathy and disinterest rise to the surface when the next logical steps are to be taken. Laws are passed in a crisis mood after a Birmingham or a Selma, but no substantial fervor survives the formal signing of legislation. The recording of the law in itself is treated as the reality of the reform."

"Justice for black people will not flow into society merely from court decisions nor from fountains of political oratory. Nor will a few token changes quell all the tempestuous yearnings of millions of disadvantaged black people. White America must recognize that justice for black people cannot be achieved without radical changes in the structure

of our society. The comfortable, the entrenched, the privileged cannot continue to tremble at the prospect of change in the status quo.

"When millions of people have been cheated for centuries, restitution is a costly process. Inferior education, poor housing, unemployment, inadequate health care—each is a bitter component of the oppression that has been our heritage. Each will require billions of dollars to correct. Justice so long deferred has accumulated interest and its cost for this society will be substantial in financial as well as human terms. This fact has not been fully grasped, because most of the gains of the past decade were obtained at bargain rates. The desegregation of public facilities cost nothing; neither did the election and appointment of a few black public officials."

"Direct action is not a substitute for work in the courts and the halls of government. Bringing about passage of a new and broad law by a city council, state legislature, or the Congress, or pleading cases before the courts of the land, does not eliminate the necessity for bringing about the mass dramatization of injustice in front of a city hall. Indeed, direct action and legal action complement one another; when skillfully employed, each becomes more effective."

"One of the most basic weapons in the fight for social justice will be the cumulative political power of the Negro. I can foresee the Negro vote becoming consistently the decisive vote in national elections."

"The hope of the world is still in dedicated minorities. The trailblazers in human, academic, scientific, and religious freedom have always been in the minority. That creative minority of whites absolutely committed to civil rights can make it clear to the larger society that vacillation and procrastination on the question of racial justice can no longer be tolerated. It will take such a small committed minority to work unrelentingly to win the uncommitted majority. Such a group may well transform America's greatest dilemma into her most glorious opportunity."

"Our hope for creative living in this world house that we have inherited lies in our ability to reestablish the moral ends of our lives in personal character and social justice. Without this spiritual and moral reawakening we shall destroy ourselves in the misuse of our own instruments."

"The deep rumbling of discontent that we hear today is the thunder of disinherited masses, rising from dungeons of oppression to the bright hills of freedom, in one majestic chorus the rising masses singing, in the words of our freedom song, 'Ain't gonna let nobody turn us around.' All over the world, like a fever, the freedom movement is spreading in the widest liberation in history. The great masses of people are determined to end the exploitation of their races and land. They are awake and moving toward their goal like a tidal wave. You can hear them rumbling in every village, street, on the docks, in the houses, among the students in the churches and at political meetings.

"These developments should not surprise any student of history. Oppressed people cannot remain oppressed forever. The yearning for freedom eventually manifests itself. The Bible tells the thrilling story of how Moses stood in Pharaoh's court centuries ago and cried, 'Let my people go.' "

"Human progress is neither automatic nor inevitable. Even a superficial look at history reveals that no social advance rolls in on the wheels of inevitability. Every step toward the goal of justice requires sacrifice, suffering, and struggle; the tireless exertions and passionate concern of dedicated individuals. Without persistent effort, time itself becomes an ally of the insurgent and primitive forces of irrational emotionalism and social destruction. This is no time for apathy or complacency. This is a time for vigorous and positive action."

FAITH
AND
RELIGION

"There is so much frustration in the world because we have relied on gods rather than God. We have genuflected before the god of science only to find that it has given us the atomic bomb, producing fears and anxieties that science can never mitigate. We have worshiped the god of pleasure only to discover that thrills play out and sensations are short-lived. We have bowed before the god of money only to learn that there are such things as love and friendship that money cannot buy and that in a world of possible depressions, stock market crashes, and bad business investments, money is a rather uncertain deity. These transitory gods are not able to save or bring happiness to the human heart. Only God is able. It is faith in Him that we must rediscover."

"Science investigates; religion interprets. Science gives man knowledge which is power; religion gives man wisdom which is control. Science deals mainly with facts; religion deals mainly with values. The two are not rivals. They are complementary. Science keeps religion from sinking into the valley of crippling irrationalism and paralyzing obscurantism. Religion prevents science from falling into the marsh of obsolete materialism and moral nihilism."

"So I say to you, seek God and discover Him and make Him a power in your life. Without Him all of our efforts turn to ashes and our sunrises into darkest nights. Without Him, life is a meaningless drama with the decisive scenes missing. But with Him we are able to rise from the fatigue of despair to the buoyancy of hope. With Him we are able to rise from the midnight of desperation to the daybreak of joy. St. Augustine was right—we were made for God and we will be restless until we find rest in Him.

"Love yourself, if that means rational, healthy, and moral self-interest. You are commanded to do that. That is the length of life. Love your neighbor as you love yourself. You are commanded to do that. That is the breadth of life. But never forget that there is a first and even greater commandment, 'Love the Lord thy God with all thy heart and all thy soul and all thy mind.' This is the height of life. And when you do this you live the complete life."

"Something should remind us once more that the great things in this universe are things that we never see. You walk out at night and look up at the beautiful stars as they bedeck the heavens like swinging lanterns of eternity, and you think you can see all. Oh, no. You can never see the law of gravitation that holds them there."

"When I speak of love I am not speaking of some sentimental and weak response. I am speaking of that force which all of the great religions have seen as the supreme unifying principle of life. Love is somehow the key that unlocks the door which leads to ultimate reality."

"Love is the most durable power in the world. This creative force, so beautifully exemplified in the life of our Christ, is the most potent instrument available in mankind's quest for peace and security."

"Worship at its best is a social experience with people of all levels of life coming together to realize their oneness and unity under God. Whenever the church, consciously or unconsciously, caters to one class it loses the spiritual force of the 'whosoever will, let him come' doctrine and is in danger of becoming little more than a social club with a thin veneer of religiosity."

"The belief that God will do everything for man is as untenable as the belief that man can do everything for himself. It, too, is based on a lack of faith. We must learn that to expect God to do everything while we do nothing is not faith but superstition."

"A religion true to its nature must also be concerned about man's social conditions. Religion deals with both earth and heaven, both time and eternity. Religion operates not only on the vertical plane but also on the horizontal. It seeks not only to integrate men with God but to integrate men with men and each man with himself. This means, at bottom, that the Christian gospel is a two-way road. On the one hand, it seeks to change the souls of men and thereby unite them with God; on the other hand, it seeks to change the environmental conditions of men so that the soul will have a chance after it is changed. Any religion that professes to be concerned with the souls of men and is not concerned with the slums that damn them, the economic conditions that strangle them, and the social conditions that cripple them is a dry-as-dust religion. Such a religion is the kind the Marxists like to see—an opiate of the people."

"Shattered dreams are a hallmark of our mortal life."

"One of the most agonizing problems within our human experience is that few, if any, of us live to see our fondest hopes fulfilled. The hopes of our childhood and the promises of our mature years are unfinished symphonies."

"If you are cut down in a movement that is designed to save the soul of a nation, then no other death could be more redemptive."

"We must somehow believe that unearned suffering is redemptive."

"We must work passionately and indefatigably to bridge the gulf between our scientific progress and our moral progress. One of the great problems of mankind is that we suffer from a poverty of the spirit which stands in glaring contrast to our scientific and technological abundance. The richer we have become materially, the poorer we have become morally and spiritually.

"Every man lives in two realms, the internal and the external. The internal is that realm of spiritual ends expressed in art, literature, morals, and religion. The external is that complex of devices, techniques, mechanisms, and instrumentalities by means of which we live. Our problem today is that we have allowed the internal to become lost in the external. We have allowed the means by which we live to outdistance the ends for which we live."

NONVIOLENCE

"I've decided that I'm going to do battle for my philosophy. You ought to believe something in life, believe that thing so fervently that you will stand up with it till the end of your days. I can't make myself believe that God wants me to hate. I'm tired of violence. And I'm not going to let my oppressor dictate to me what method I must use. We have a power, power that can't be found in Molotov cocktails, but we do have a power. Power that cannot be found in bullets and guns, but we have a power. It is a power as old as the insights of Jesus of Nazareth and as modern as the techniques of Mahatma Gandhi."

"If humanity is to progress, Gandhi is inescapable. He lived, thought, and acted, inspired by the vision of humanity evolving toward a world of peace and harmony. We may ignore him at our own risk."

"I am convinced that if we succumb to the temptation to use violence in our struggle for freedom, unborn generations will be the recipients of a long and desolate night of bitterness, and our chief legacy to them will be a never-ending reign of chaos."

"I've seen too much hate to want to hate, myself, and I've seen hate on the faces of too many sheriffs, too many White Citizens Councilors, and too many Klansmen of the South to want to hate, myself; and every time I see it, I say to myself, hate is too great a burden to bear. Somehow we must be able to stand up before our most bitter opponents and say: 'We shall match your capacity to inflict suffering by our capacity to endure suffering. We will meet your physical force with soul force. Do to us what you will and we will still love you. We cannot in all good conscience obey your unjust laws and abide by the unjust system, because noncooperation with evil is as much a moral obligation as is cooperation with good, and so throw us in jail and we will still love you. Bomb our homes and threaten our children, and, as difficult as it is, we will still love you. Send your hooded perpetrators of violence into our communities at the midnight hour and drag us out on some wayside road and leave us half-dead as you beat us, and we will still love you. Send your propaganda agents around the country and make it appear that we are not fit, culturally and otherwise, for integration, but we'll still love you. But be assured that we'll wear you down by our capacity to suffer, and one day we will win our freedom. We will not only win freedom for ourselves, we will so appeal to your heart and conscience that we will win you in the process, and our victory will be a double victory.'

"If there is to be peace on earth and good will toward men, we must finally believe in the ultimate morality of the universe, and believe that all reality hinges on moral foundations."

"Violence as a way of achieving racial justice is both impractical and immoral. It is impractical because it is a descending spiral ending in destruction for all. The old law of an eye for an eye leaves everybody blind. It is immoral because it seeks to humiliate the opponent rather than win his understanding; it seeks to annihilate rather than to convert. Violence is immoral because it thrives on hatred rather than love. It destroys community and makes brotherhood impossible. It leaves society in monologue rather than dialogue. Violence ends by defeating itself. It creates bitterness in the survivors and brutality in the destroyers."

"When one tries to pin down advocates of violence as to what acts would be effective, the answers are blatantly illogical. Sometimes they talk of overthrowing racist state and local governments. They fail to see that no internal revolution has ever succeeded in overthrowing a government by violence unless the government had already lost the allegiance and effective control of its armed forces. Anyone in his right mind knows that this will not happen in the United States. In a violent racial situation, the power structure has the local police, the state troopers, the national guard, and finally the army to call on, all of which are predominately white."

I HEREBY PLEDGE MYSELF—MY PERSON AND BODY—TO THE
NONVIOLENT MOVEMENT. THEREFORE I WILL KEEP THE
FOLLOWING TEN COMMANDMENTS: *

1. MEDITATE daily on the teachings and life of Jesus.
2. REMEMBER always that the nonviolent movement in
   Birmingham seeks justice and reconciliation—not victory.
3. WALK and TALK in the manner of love, for God is love.
4. PRAY daily to be used by God in order that all men might
   be free.
5. SACRIFICE personal wishes in order that all men might be
   free.
6. OBSERVE with both friend and foe the ordinary rules of
   courtesy.
7. SEEK to perform regular service for others and for the
   world.
8. REFRAIN from the violence of fist, tongue, or heart.
9. STRIVE to be in good spiritual and bodily health.
10. FOLLOW the directions of the movement and of the captain
    on a demonstration.

I sign this pledge, having seriously considered what I do and
with the determination and will to persevere.

Name_____

Address_____

Phone_____

Nearest Relative_____

Address_____

Besides demonstrations, I could also help the movement by:
(Circle the proper items)

Run errands, Drive my car, Fix food for volunteers, Clerical work,
Make phone calls, Answer phones, Mimeograph, Type, Print signs,
Distribute leaflets.

ALABAMA CHRISTIAN MOVEMENT FOR HUMAN RIGHTS
BIRMINGHAM Affiliate of S.C.L.C.
505½ North 17th Street
F. L. Shuttlesworth, President

* Pledge signed by volunteers for sit-in demonstrations to protest
segregated eating facilities in Birmingham, Alabama, in 1963.

"Fortunately, history does not pose problems without eventually producing solutions. The disenchanted, the disadvantaged, and the disinherited seem, at times of deep crisis, to summon up some sort of genius that enables them to perceive and capture the appropriate weapons to carve out their destiny. Such was the peaceable weapon of nonviolent direct action, which materialized almost overnight to inspire the Negro and was seized in his outstretched hands with a powerful grip.

"Nonviolent action, the Negro saw, was the way to supplement—not replace—the process of change through legal recourse. It was the way to divest himself of passivity without arraying himself in vindictive force. Acting in concert with fellow Negroes to assert himself as a citizen, he would embark on a militant program to demand the rights which were his: in the streets, on the buses, in the stores, the parks, and other public facilities.

"The religious tradition of the Negro had shown him that the nonviolent resistance of the early Christians had constituted a moral offensive of such overriding power that it shook the Roman Empire. American history had taught him that nonviolence in the form of boycotts and protests had confounded the British monarchy and laid the basis for freeing the colonies from unjust domination. Within his own century, the nonviolent ethic of Mahatma Gandhi and his followers had muzzled the guns of the British empire in India and freed more than three hundred and fifty million people from colonialism."

"Mass civil disobedience as a new stage of struggle can transmute the deep rage of the ghetto into a constructive and creative force. To dislocate the functioning of a city without destroying it can be more effective than a riot because it can be longer-lasting, costly to the larger society, but not wantonly destructive. Finally, it is a device of social action that is more difficult for the government to quell by superior force.

"The limitation of riots, moral questions aside, is that they cannot win and their participants know it. Hence, rioting is not revolutionary but reactionary because it invites defeat. It involves an emotional catharsis, but it must be followed by a sense of futility."

"The argument that nonviolence is a coward's refuge lost its force as its heroic and often perilous acts uttered their wordless but convincing rebuttal in Montgomery, in the sit-ins, on the freedom rides, and finally in Birmingham.

"There is a powerful motivation when a suppressed people enlist in an army that marches under the banner of nonviolence. A nonviolent army has a magnificent universal quality. To join an army that trains its adherents in the methods of violence, you must be of a certain age. But in Birmingham, some of the most valued foot soldiers were youngsters ranging from elementary pupils to teenage high school and college students."

"Compassion and nonviolence help us to see the enemy's point of view, to hear his questions, to know his assessment of ourselves. For from his view we may indeed see the basic weaknesses of our own condition, and if we are mature, we may learn and grow and profit from the wisdom of the brothers who are called the opposition."

"I am mindful that only yesterday in Birmingham, Alabama,* our children, crying out for brotherhood, were answered with fire hoses, snarling dogs, and even death. I am mindful that only yesterday in Philadelphia, Mississippi, young people seeking to secure the right to vote were brutalized and murdered. Therefore I must ask why this prize is awarded to a movement which is beleaguered and committed to unrelenting struggle; to a movement which has not won the very peace and brotherhood which is the essence of the Nobel Prize. After contemplation I conclude that this award, which I receive on behalf of the movement, is a profound recognition that nonviolence is the answer to the crucial political and racial questions of our time—the need for man to overcome oppression without resorting to violence."

* From the Nobel Peace Prize acceptance speech, December 10, 1964.

"Admittedly, nonviolence in the truest sense is not a strategy that one uses simply because it is expedient at the moment; nonviolence is ultimately a way of life that men live by because of the sheer morality of its claim. But even granting this, the willingness to use nonviolence as a technique is a step forward. For he who goes this far is more likely to adopt nonviolence later as a way of life."

"The principle of nonviolent resistance seeks to reconcile the truths of two opposites—acquiescence and violence—while avoiding the extremes and immoralities of both. The nonviolent resister agrees with the person who acquiesces that one should not be physically aggressive toward his opponent; but he balances the equation by agreeing with the person of violence that evil must be resisted. He avoids the nonresistance of the former and the violent resistance of the latter. With nonviolent resistance, no individual or group need submit to any wrong, nor need anyone resort to violence in order to right a wrong."

"The nonviolent approach does not immediately change the heart of the oppressor. It first does something to the hearts and souls of those committed to it. It gives them new self-respect; it calls up resources of strength and courage that they did not know they had. Finally it reaches the opponent and so stirs his conscience that reconciliation becomes a reality."

PEACE

"The past is prophetic in that it asserts loudly that wars are poor chisels for carving out peaceful tomorrows. One day we must come to see that peace is not merely a distant goal that we seek, but a means by which we arrive at that goal. We must pursue peaceful ends through peaceful means. How much longer must we play at deadly war games before we heed the plaintive pleas of the unnumbered dead and maimed of past wars?"

"True peace is not merely the absence of tension; it is the presence of justice."

"Now let me say that the next thing we must be concerned about if we are to have peace on earth and good will toward men is the nonviolent affirmation of the sacredness of all human life. Every man is somebody because he is a child of God."

"The church cannot be silent while mankind faces the threat of nuclear annihilation. If the church is true to her mission, she must call for an end to the arms race."

"One of the most persistent ambiguities that we face is that everybody talks about peace as a goal. However, it does not take sharpest-eyed sophistication to discern that while everybody talks about peace, peace has become practically nobody's business among the power-wielders. Many men cry Peace! Peace! but they refuse to do the things that make for peace.

"The large power blocs of the world talk passionately of pursuing peace while burgeoning defense budgets bulge, enlarging already awesome armies, and devising even more devastating weapons. Call the roll of those who sing the glad tidings of peace and one's ears will be surprised by the responding sounds. The heads of all of the nations issue clarion calls for peace yet these destiny determiners come accompanied by a band and a brigade of national choristers, each bearing unsheathed swords rather than olive branches."

"I do not minimize the complexity of the problems that need to be faced in achieving disarmament and peace. But I am convinced that we shall not have the will, the courage, and the insight to deal with such matters unless in this field we are prepared to undergo a mental and spiritual reevaluation, a change of focus which will enable us to see that the things that seem most real and powerful are indeed now unreal and have come under sentence of death.

"It is not enough to say, 'We must not wage war.' It is necessary to love peace and sacrifice for it. We must concentrate not merely on the eradication of war but on the affirmation of peace.

"So we must see that peace represents a sweeter music, a cosmic melody that is far superior to the discords of war. Somehow we must transform the dynamics of the world power struggle from the nuclear arms race, which no one can win, to a creative contest to harness man's genius for the purpose of making peace and prosperity a reality for all the nations of the world. In short, we must shift the arms race into a 'peace race.' If we have the will and determination to mount such a peace offensive, we will unlock hitherto tightly sealed doors of hope and bring new light into the dark chambers of pessimism."

"If we assume that life is worth living and that man has a right to survival, then we must find an alternative to war. In a day when vehicles hurtle through outer space and guided ballistic missiles carve highways of death through the stratosphere, no nation can claim victory in war."

"We will never have peace in the world until men everywhere recognize that ends are not cut off from means, because the means represent the ideal in the making, and the end in process. Ultimately you can't reach good ends through evil means, because the means represent the seed and the end represents the tree."

"The physical casualties of the war in Vietnam are not alone the catastrophies. The casualities of principles and values are equally disastrous and injurious. Indeed, they are ultimately more harmful because they are self-perpetuating. If the casualties of principle are not healed, the physical casualties will continue to mount."

"We must have patience. We must be willing to understand why many of the young nations will have to pass through the same extremism, revolution, and aggression that formed our own history. Every new government confronts overwhelming problems. During the days when they were struggling to remove the yoke of colonialism, there was a kind of preexistent unity of purpose that kept things moving in one solid direction. But as soon as independence emerges, all the grim problems of life confront them with stark realism: the lack of capital, the strangulating poverty, the uncontrollable birth rates and, above all, the high aspirational level of their own people. The postcolonial period is more difficult and precarious than the colonial struggle itself.

"The West must also understand that its economic growth took place under rather propitious circumstances. Most of the Western nations were relatively underpopulated when they surged forward economically, and they were greatly endowed with the iron ore and coal that were needed for launching industry. Most of the young governments of the world today have come into being without these advantages, and, above all, they confront staggering problems of overpopulation. There is no possible way for them to make it without aid and assistance."

"It is time for all people of conscience to call upon America to return to her true home of brotherhood and peaceful pursuits. We cannot remain silent as our nation engages in one of history's most cruel and senseless wars. During these days of human travail we must encourage creative dissenters. We need them because the thunder of their fearless voices will be the only sound stronger than the blasts of bombs and the clamor of war hysteria.

"Those of us who love peace must organize as effectively as the war hawks. As they spread the propaganda of war, we must spread the propaganda of peace. We must combine the fervor of the civil rights movement with the peace movement. We must demonstrate, teach, and preach, until the very foundations of our nation are shaken. We must work unceasingly to lift this nation that we love to a higher destiny, to a new plateau of compassion, to a more noble expression of humaneness.

"I have tried to be honest. To be honest is to confront the truth. However unpleasant and inconvenient the truth may be, I believe we must expose and face it if we are to achieve a better quality of American life."

"We are now faced with the fact that tomorrow is today. We are confronted with the fierce urgency of *now*. In this unfolding conundrum of life and history there is such a thing as being too late. Procrastination is still the thief of time. Life often leaves us standing bare, naked, and dejected with a lost opportunity. The 'tide in the affairs of men' does not remain at the flood; it ebbs. We may cry out desperately for time to pause in her passage, but time is deaf to every plea and rushes on. Over the bleached bones and jumbled residues of numerous civilizations are written the pathetic words: 'Too late.' There is an invisible book of life that faithfully records our vigilance or our neglect. 'The moving finger writes, and having writ moves on. . . .' We still have a choice today: nonviolent coexistence or violent coannihilation. This may well be mankind's last chance to choose between chaos and community."

"Hatred and bitterness can never cure the disease of fear; only love can do that. Hatred paralyzes life; love releases it. Hatred confuses life; love harmonizes it. Hatred darkens life; love illumines it."

"I refuse to accept the cynical notion that nation after nation must spiral down a militaristic stairway into the hell of thermonuclear destruction. I believe that unarmed truth and unconditional love will have the final word in reality. This is why right temporarily defeated is stronger than evil triumphant.

"I believe that even amid today's mortar bursts and whining bullets, there is still hope for a brighter tomorrow. I believe that wounded justice, lying prostrate on the blood-flowing streets of our nations, can be lifted from this dust of shame to reign supreme among the children of men.

"I still believe that one day mankind will bow before the altars of God and be crowned triumphant over war and bloodshed, and nonviolent redemptive good will will proclaim the rule of the land. 'And the lion and the lamb shall lie down together and every man shall sit under his own vine and fig tree and none shall be afraid.' I still believe that we shall overcome."

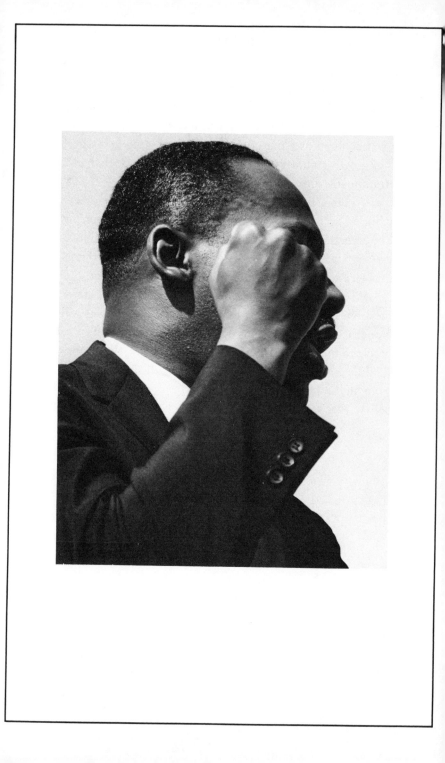

"I've Been to the Mountain Top"

... We have been forced to a point where we're going to have to grapple with the problems that men have been trying to grapple with through history, but the demands didn't force them to do it. Survival demands that we grapple with them. Men, for years now, have been talking about war and peace. But now no longer can they just talk about it. It is no longer a choice between violence and nonviolence in this world, it's nonviolence or nonexistence.

That is where we are today. And also in the human rights revolution, if something isn't done, and in a hurry, to bring the colored peoples of the world out of their long years of poverty, their long years of hurt and neglect, the whole world is doomed.

... If I lived in China or even Russia, or any totalitarian country, maybe I could understand some of these illegal injunctions. Maybe I could understand the denial of certain basic First Amendment privileges, because they hadn't committed themselves to that over there. But somewhere I read of the freedom of assembly. Somewhere I read of the freedom of speech. Somewhere I read of the freedom of the press. Somewhere I read that the greatness of America is the right to protest for right. And so, just as I say, we aren't going to let any dog or water hose turn us around. We aren't going to let any injunction turn us around. We are going on.

... Let us rise up tonight with a greater readiness. Let us stand with a greater determination. And let us move on in these powerful days, these days of challenge, to make America what it ought to be. We have an opportunity to make a better nation. And I want to thank God, once more, for allowing me to be here with you.

. . . I don't know what will happen now. We've got some difficult days ahead. But it really doesn't matter with me now, because I've been to the mountain top. And I don't mind. Like anybody, I would like to live a long life; longevity has its place. But I'm not concerned about that now. I just want to do God's will. And He's allowed me to go up to the mountain. And I've looked over. And I've seen the promised land. I may not get there with you. But I want you to know tonight that we as a people will get to the promised land. And I'm happy tonight, I'm not worried about anything. I'm not fearing any man. Mine eyes have seen the glory of the coming of the Lord.

April 3, 1968
Memphis, Tennessee
Excerpt from Dr. King's last speech, before he was assassinated on April 4.

"I Have a Dream"

... I say to you today, my friends, so even though we face the difficulties of today and tomorrow, I still have a dream. It is a dream deeply rooted in the American dream.

I have a dream that one day this nation will rise up and live out the true meaning of its creed: "We hold these truths to be self-evident; that all men are created equal."

I have a dream that one day, on the red hills of Georgia, sons of former slaves and the sons of former slaveowners will be able to sit down together at the table of brotherhood.

I have a dream that one day even the state of Mississippi, a state sweltering with the heat of injustice, sweltering with the heat of oppression, will be transformed into an oasis of freedom and justice.

I have a dream that my four little children will one day live in a nation where they will not be judged by the color of their skin but by the content of their character.

I have a dream today.

I have a dream that one day, down in Alabama, with its vicious racists, with its governor having his lips dripping with the words of interposition and nullification, one day right there in Alabama, little black boys and black girls will be able to join hands with little white boys and white girls and walk together as sisters and brothers.

I have a dream today.

I have a dream that one day "every valley shall be

exalted, every hill and mountain shall be made low, the rough places will be made plains, and the crooked places will be made straight, and the glory of the Lord shall be revealed, and all flesh shall see it together."

This is our hope. This is the faith that I go back to the South with. With this faith we will be able to hew out of the mountain of despair a stone of hope. With this faith we will be able to transform the jangling discords of our nation into a beautiful symphony of brotherhood. With this faith we will be able to work together, to pray together, to struggle together, to stand up for freedom together, knowing that we will be free one day.

And this will be the day. This will be the day when all of God's children will be able to sing with new meaning "My country 'tis of thee, sweet land of liberty, of thee I sing. Land where my fathers died, land of the pilgrim's pride, from every mountainside, let freedom ring."

And if America is to be a great nation this must become true. So let freedom ring from the prodigious hilltops of New Hampshire. Let freedom ring from the mighty mountains of New York. Let freedom ring from the heightening Alleghenies of Pennsylvania!

Let freedom ring from the snowcapped Rockies of Colorado!

Let freedom ring from the curvaceous slopes of California!

But not only that; let freedom ring from Stone Mountain of Georgia! Let freedom ring from Lookout Mountain of Tennessee.

Let freedom ring from every hill and molehill of Mississippi. From every mountainside, let freedom ring.

And when this happens, and when we allow freedom to ring, when we let it ring from every village and every hamlet, from every state and every city, we will be able to speed up that day when all of God's children, black men and white men, Jews and Gentiles, Protestants and Catholics, will be able to join hands and sing in the words of that old Negro spiritual, "Free at last! Free at last! Thank God almighty, we are free at last!"

August 28, 1963
Washington, D.C.
Excerpt from the speech given at the March on Washington

PROCLAMATION OF
MARTIN LUTHER KING, JR. DAY
BY THE PRESIDENT
OF THE UNITED STATES

Public Law 98–144
98th Congress

An Act

To amend title 5, United States Code, to make the birthday of Martin
Luther King, Jr., a legal public holiday.

*Be it enacted by the Senate and House of Representatives of the
United States of America in Congress assembled,* That section 6103(a)
of title 5, United States Code, is amended by inserting immediately
below the item relating to New Year's Day the following:

"Birthday of Martin Luther King, Jr., the third Monday in
January.".

SEC. 2. The amendment made by the first section of this Act shall
take effect on the first January 1 that occurs after the two-year
period following the date of the enactment of this Act.

Approved November 2, 1983.

MARTIN LUTHER KING, JR. DAY, 1986

BY THE PRESIDENT OF
THE UNITED STATES OF AMERICA

A PROCLAMATION

This year marks the first observance of the birthday of
Dr. Martin Luther King, Jr. as a national holiday. It is a time for
rejoicing and reflecting. We rejoice because, in his short life,
Dr. King, by his preaching, his example, and his leadership, helped
to move us closer to the ideals on which America was founded.
We reflect on his words and his works. Dr. King's was truly a
prophetic voice that reached out over the chasms of hostility,
prejudice, ignorance, and fear to touch the conscience of America.
He challenged us to make real the promise of America as a
land of freedom, equality, opportunity, and brotherhood.

Although Dr. King was an uncompromising champion of
nonviolence, he was often the victim of violence. And, as we
know, a shameful act of violence cut short his life before he had
reached his fortieth birthday.

His story is well-known. As a 26–year–old minister of the
Gospel, Dr. King led a protest boycott of a bus company that
segregated blacks, treating them as second–class citizens. At the
very outset he admonished all those who would join in the protest
that "our actions must be guided by the deepest principles of our
Christian faith. Love must be our regulating ideal." Otherwise, he
warned, "our protest will end up as a meaningless drama on the
stage of history...shrouded with ugly garments of shame." Dr.
King's unshakable faith inspired others to resist the temptation to
hate and fear. His protest became a triumph of courage and love.

Almost 30 years ago, on January 30, 1956, Dr. King stood
amid the broken glass and splinters of his bombed-out front porch
and calmed an angry crowd clamoring for vengeance. "We cannot
solve this problem through retaliatory violence," he told them. Dr.
King steadfastly opposed both the timid and those who counselled
violence. To the former, he preached that "true peace is not merely

the absence of tension; it is the presence of justice." To the latter, he said that "in the process of gaining our rightful place we must not be guilty of wrongful deeds."

Dr. King's activism was rooted in the true patriotism that cherishes America's ideals and strives to narrow the gap between those ideals and reality. He took his stand, he once explained, "because of my love for America and the sublime principles of liberty and equality on which she is founded." He wanted "to transform the jangling discords of our Nation into a beautiful symphony of brotherhood."

The majesty of his message, the dignity of his bearing, and the righteousness of his cause are a lasting legacy. In a few short years he changed America for all time. He made it possible for our Nation to move closer to the ideals set forth in our Declaration of Independence: that all people are created equal and are endowed with inalienable rights that government has the duty to respect and protect.

Twenty-three years ago, Dr. King spoke to a quarter of a million Americans gathered near the Lincoln Memorial in Washington—and to tens of millions more watching on television. There he held up his dream for America like a bright banner:

"I have a dream," he said, "that my four little children will one day live in a Nation where they will not be judged by the color of their skin, but by the content of their character....This will be the day when all of God's children will be able to sing with new meaning, 'My country 'tis of thee, sweet land of liberty, of thee I sing.'"

Let all Americans continue to carry forward the banner that 18 years ago fell from Dr. King's hands. Today, all over America, libraries, hospitals, parks, and thoroughfares proudly bear his name. His likeness appears on more than 100 postage stamps issued by dozens of nations around the globe. Today we honor him with speeches and monuments. But let us do more. Let all

Americans of every race and creed and color work together to build in this blessed land a shining city of brotherhood, justice, and harmony. This is the monument Dr. King would have wanted most of all.

By Public Law 98–144, the third Monday in January of each year has been designated as a public holiday in honor of the "Birthday of Martin Luther King, Jr."

NOW, THEREFORE, I, RONALD REAGAN, President of the United States of America, do hereby proclaim Monday, January 20, 1986, as Martin Luther King, Jr. Day.

IN WITNESS WHEREOF, I have hereunto set my hand this eighteenth day of January, in the year of our Lord nineteen hundred and eighty–six, and of the Independence of the United States of America the two hundred and tenth.

RONALD REAGAN

CHRONOLOGY

1929

January 15   Martin Luther King, Jr., is born to Reverend and Mrs. Martin Luther King, Sr. (the former Alberta Christine Williams), in Atlanta, Georgia.

1935–1944   King attends David T. Howard Elementary School, Atlanta University Laboratory School, and Booker T. Washington High School. He passes the entrance examination to Morehouse College (Atlanta) without graduating from high school.

1947   King is licensed to preach and becomes assistant to his father, who is pastor of the Ebenezer Baptist Church, Atlanta.

1948

February 25   King is ordained to the Baptist ministry.

June   King graduates from Morehouse College with a B.A. degree in sociology.

September   King enters Crozer Theological Seminary, Chester, Pennsylvania. After hearing Dr. A. J. Muste and Dr. Mordecai W. Johnson preach on the life and teachings of Mahatma Gandhi, he begins to study Gandhi seriously.

1951

June   King graduates from Crozer with a B.D. degree.

1953

June 18   King marries Coretta Scott in Marion, Alabama.

1954

May 17   The Supreme Court of the United States rules unanimously in *Brown* vs. *Board of Education* that racial segregation in public schools is unconstitutional.

1954 (*continued*)

October 31   King is installed by Reverend Martin Luther King, Sr., as the twentieth pastor of the Dexter Avenue Church, Montgomery.

1955

June 5   King receives a Ph.D. degree in Systematic Theology from Boston University.

November 17   The Kings' first child, Yolanda Denise, is born in Montgomery.

December 1   Mrs. Rosa Parks, a forty-two-year-old Montgomery seamstress, refuses to relinquish her bus seat to a white man and is arrested.

December 5   The first day of the bus boycott. The trial of Mrs. Parks. A meeting of movement leaders is held. Dr. King is unanimously elected president of an organization named the Montgomery Improvement Association, a name proposed by Reverend Ralph Abernathy.

December 10   The Montgomery Bus Company suspends service in black neighborhoods.

1956

January 26   Dr. King is arrested on a charge of traveling thirty miles per hour in a twenty-five-mile-per-hour zone in Montgomery. He is released on his own recognizance.

January 30   A bomb is thrown onto the porch of Dr. King's Montgomery home. Mrs. King and Mrs. Roscoe Williams, wife of a church member, are in the house with baby Yolanda Denise; no one is injured.

February 2   A suit is filed in federal district court asking that Montgomery's travel segregation laws be declared unconstitutional.

February 21   Dr. King is indicted with other figures in the Montgomery bus boycott on the charge of being party to a conspiracy to hinder and prevent the operation of business without "just or legal cause."

June 4	A United States district court rules that racial segregation on city bus lines is unconstitutional.
August 10	Dr. King is a speaker before the platform committee of the Democratic Party in Chicago.
October 30	Mayor Gayle of Montgomery instructs the city's legal department "to file such proceedings as it may deem proper to stop the operation of car pools and transportation systems growing out of the boycott."
November 13	The United States Supreme Court affirms the decision of the three-judge district court in declaring unconstitutional Alabama's state and local laws requiring segregation on buses.
December 20	Federal injunctions prohibiting segregation on buses are served on city and bus company officials in Montgomery. Injunctions are also served on state officials.
December 21	Montgomery buses are integrated.

1957
January 27	An unexploded bomb is discovered on the front porch of the Kings' house.
February	The Southern Christian Leadership Conference (SCLC) is founded. Dr. King is elected its president.
February 18	*Time* magazine puts Dr. King on its cover.
May 17	Dr. King delivers a speech for the Prayer Pilgrimage for Freedom celebrating the third anniversary of the Supreme Court's desegregation decision. The speech, entitled "Give Us the Ballot," is given at the Lincoln Memorial, Washington, D.C.
June 13	Dr. King has a conference with the vice-president of the United States, Richard M. Nixon.

1957 (*continued*)

September President Dwight D. Eisenhower federalizes the Arkansas National Guard to escort nine Negro students to an all-white high school in Little Rock, Arkansas.

September 9 The first civil rights act since Reconstruction is passed by Congress, creating the Civil Rights Commission and the Civil Rights Division of the Department of Justice.

October 23 A second child, Martin Luther III, is born to Dr. and Mrs. King.

1958

June 23 Dr. King, along with Roy Wilkins of the NAACP, A. Philip Randolph, and Lester Granger, meets with President Dwight D. Eisenhower.

September 3 Dr. King is arrested on a charge of loitering (later changed to "failure to obey an officer") in the vicinity of the Montgomery Recorder's Court. He is released on $100 bond.

September 4 Dr. King is convicted after pleading "not guilty" on the charge of failure to obey an officer. The fine is paid almost immediately, over Dr. King's objection, by Montgomery Police Commissioner Clyde C. Sellers.

September 17 Dr. King's book *Stride Toward Freedom: The Montgomery Story* is published by Harper & Row.

September 20 Dr. King is stabbed in the chest by Mrs. Izola Curry, forty-two, who is subsequently alleged to be mentally deranged. The stabbing occurs in the heart of Harlem while Dr. King is autographing his recently published book. His condition is said to be serious but not critical.

1959

January 30 Dr. King meets with Walter Reuther, president of the United Auto Workers union, in Detroit.

February 2–
March 10 Dr. and Mrs. King spend a month in India studying Gandhi's techniques of nonviolence, as guests of Prime Minister Nehru.

1960

January 24	The King family moves to Atlanta. Dr. King becomes copastor, with his father, of the Ebenezer Baptist Church.
February 1	The first lunch-counter sit-in to desegregate eating facilities is held by students in Greensboro, North Carolina.
February 17	A warrant is issued for Dr. King's arrest on charges that he had falsified his 1956 and 1958 Alabama state income tax returns.
April 15	The Student Nonviolent Coordinating Committee (SNCC) is founded to coordinate student protest at Shaw University, Raleigh, North Carolina, on a temporary basis. (It is to become a permanent organization in October 1960.) Dr. King and James Lawson are the keynote speakers at the Shaw University founding.
May 28	Dr. King is acquitted of the tax evasion charge by an all-white jury in Montgomery.
June 10	Dr. King and A. Philip Randolph announce plans for picketing both the Republican and Democratic national conventions.
June 24	Dr. King has a conference with John F. Kennedy, candidate for president of the United States, about racial matters.
October 19	Dr. King is arrested at an Atlanta sit-in and is jailed on a charge of violating the state's trespass law.
October 22–27	The Atlanta charges are dropped. All jailed demonstrators are released except for Dr. King, who is ordered held on a charge of violating a probated sentence in a traffic arrest case. He is transferred to the DeKalb County Jail in Decatur, Georgia, and is then transferred to the Reidsville State Prison. He is released from the Reidsville State Prison on a $2,000 bond.

1961

January 30	A third child, Dexter Scott, is born to Dr. and Mrs. King in Atlanta.

1961 (*continued*)

May 4	The first group of Freedom Riders, intent on integrating interstate buses, leaves Washington, D.C., by Greyhound bus. The group, organized by the Congress for Racial Equality (CORE), leaves shortly after the Supreme Court has outlawed segregation in interstate transportation terminals. The bus is burned outside of Anniston, Alabama, on May 14. A mob beats the Riders upon their arrival in Birmingham. The Riders are arrested in Jackson, Mississippi, and spend forty to sixty days in Parchman Penitentiary.
December 15	Dr. King arrives in Albany, Georgia, in response to a call from Dr. W. G. Anderson, the leader of the Albany Movement to desegregate public facilities, which began in January 1961.
December 16	Dr. King is arrested at an Albany demonstration. He is charged with obstructing the sidewalk and parading without a permit.

1962

February 27	Dr. King is tried and convicted for leading the December march in Albany.
May 2	Dr. King is invited to join the Birmingham protests.
July 27	Dr. King is arrested at an Albany city hall prayer vigil and jailed on charges of failure to obey a police officer, obstructing the sidewalk, and disorderly conduct.
September 20	James Meredith makes his first attempt to enroll at the University of Mississippi. He is actually enrolled by Supreme Court order and is escorted onto the Oxford, Mississippi, campus by U.S. marshals on October 1, 1962.
October 16	Dr. King meets with President John F. Kennedy at the White House for a one-hour conference.

1963

March 28	The Kings' fourth child, Bernice Albertine, is born.
March–April	Sit-in demonstrations are held in Birmingham to protest segregation of eating facilities. Dr. King is arrested during a demonstration.
April 16	Dr. King writes the "Letter from Birmingham Jail" while imprisoned for demonstrating.
May 3, 4, 5	Eugene ("Bull") Connor, director of public safety of Birmingham, orders the use of police dogs and fire hoses upon the marching protestors (young adults and children).
May 20	The Supreme Court of the United States rules Birmingham's segregation ordinances unconstitutional.
June	Dr. King's book *Strength to Love* is published by Harper & Row.
June 11	Governor George C. Wallace tries to stop the court-ordered integration of the University of Alabama by "standing in the schoolhouse door" and personally refusing entrance to black students and Justice Department officials. President John F. Kennedy then federalizes the Alabama National Guard, and Governor Wallace removes himself from blocking the entrance of the Negro students.
June 12	Medgar Evers, NAACP leader in Jackson, Mississippi, is assassinated at his home in the early-morning darkness, by a rifle bullet. His memorial service is held in Jackson on June 15 and he is buried in Arlington National Cemetery, Washington, D.C., on June 19.
August 28	The March on Washington, the first large integrated protest march, is held in Washington, D.C. Dr. King delivers his "I Have a Dream" speech on the steps of the Lincoln Memorial, and afterward he and other civil rights leaders meet with President John F. Kennedy in the White House.

1963 (*continued*)

September 2–10 Governor Wallace orders the Alabama state troopers to stop the court-ordered integration of Alabama's elementary and high schools until he is enjoined by court injunction from doing so. By September 10 specific schools are actually integrated by court order.

November 22 President Kennedy is assassinated in Dallas, Texas.

1964

Summer COFO (Council of Federated Organizations) initiates the Mississippi Summer Project, a voter-registration drive organized and run by black and white students.

May–June Dr. King joins other SCLC workers in demonstrations for the integration of public accommodations in St. Augustine, Florida. He is jailed.

June Dr. King's book *Why We Can't Wait* is published by Harper & Row.

June 21 Three civil rights workers—James Chaney (black) and Andrew Goodman and Michael Schwerner (white)—are reported missing after a short trip to Philadelphia, Mississippi.

July 2 Dr. King attends the signing of the Public Accommodations Bill, part of the Civil Rights Act of 1964, by President Lyndon B. Johnson in the White House.

July 18–23 Riots occur in Harlem. One black man is killed.

August Riots occur in New Jersey, Illinois, and Pennsylvania.

August 4 The bodies of civil rights workers James Chaney, Andrew Goodman, and Michael Schwerner are discovered by FBI agents buried near the town of Philadelphia, Mississippi. Neshoba County Sheriff Rainey and his deputy, Cecil Price, are allegedly implicated in the murders.

September	Dr. King and Reverend Ralph Abernathy visit West Berlin at the invitation of Mayor Willy Brandt.
September 18	Dr. King has an audience with Pope Paul VI at the Vatican.
December 10	Dr. King receives the Nobel Peace Prize in Oslo, Norway.

1965

February 21	Malcolm X, leader of the Organization of Afro-American Unity and former Black Muslim leader, is murdered by blacks in New York City.
March 7	A group of marching demonstrators (from SNCC and SCLC) led by SCLC's Hosea Williams are beaten when crossing the Edmund Pettus Bridge on their planned march to Montgomery, Alabama, from Selma, Alabama, by state highway patrolmen under the direction of Al Lingo and sheriff's deputies under the leadership of Jim Clark. An order by Governor Wallace had prohibited the march.
March 9	Unitarian minister James Reeb is beaten by four white segregationists in Selma and dies two days later.
March 15	President Johnson addresses the nation and Congress. He describes the voting rights bill he will submit to Congress in two days and uses the slogan of the civil rights movement, "We Shall Overcome."
March 16	Black and white demonstrators are beaten by sheriff's deputies and police on horseback in Montgomery.
March 21–25	Over three thousand protest marchers leave Selma for a march to Montgomery, protected by federal troops. They are joined along the way by a total of twenty-five thousand marchers. Upon reaching the Capitol they hear an address by Dr. King.

1965 (*continued*)

March 25 Mrs. Viola Liuzzo, wife of a Detroit Teamsters Union business agent, is shot and killed while driving a carload of marchers back to Selma.

July Dr. King visits Chicago. SCLC joins with the Coordinating Council of Community Organizations (CCCO), led by Al Raby, in the Chicago Project.

August–December In Alabama, SCLC spearheads voter registration campaigns in Greene, Wilcox, and Eutaw counties, and in the cities of Montgomery and Birmingham.

August 6 The 1965 Voting Rights Act is signed by President Johnson.

August 11–16 In Watts, the black ghetto of Los Angeles, riots leave thirty-five dead, of whom twenty-eight are black.

1966

February Dr. King rents an apartment in the black ghetto of Chicago.

February 23 Dr. King meets with Elijah Muhammad, leader of the Black Muslims, in Chicago.

March Dr. King takes over a Chicago slum building and is sued by its owner.

March 25 The Supreme Court of the United States rules any poll tax unconstitutional.

Spring Dr. King makes a tour of Alabama to help elect black candidates.

Spring The Alabama primary is held, the first time since Reconstruction that blacks have voted in any numbers.

May 16 An antiwar statement by Dr. King is read at a large Washington rally to protest the war in Vietnam. Dr. King agrees to serve as cochairman of Clergy and Laymen Concerned about Vietnam.

June	Stokely Carmichael and Willie Ricks (SNCC) use the slogan "Black Power" in public for the first time, before reporters in Greenwood, Mississippi.
June 6	James Meredith is shot soon after beginning his 220-mile "March Against Fear" from Memphis, Tennessee, to Jackson, Mississippi.
July 10	Dr. King launches a drive to make Chicago an "open city" in regard to housing.
August 5	Dr. King is stoned in Chicago as he leads a march through crowds of angry whites in the Gage Park section of Chicago's southwest side.
September	SCLC launches a project with the aim of integrating schools in Grenada, Mississippi.
Fall	SCLC initiates the Alabama Citizen Education Project in Wilcox County.

1967

January	Dr. King writes his book *Where Do We Go from Here?* while in Jamaica.
March 12	Alabama is ordered to desegregate all public schools.
March 25	Dr. King attacks the government's Vietnam policy in a speech at the Chicago Coliseum.
April 4	Dr. King makes a statement about the war in Vietnam, "Beyond Vietnam," at the Riverside Church, New York City.
May 10–11	One black student is killed in rioting on the campus of all-Negro Jackson State College, Jackson, Mississippi.
July 6	The Justice Department reports that more than 50 percent of all eligible black voters are registered in Mississippi, Georgia, Alabama, Louisiana, and South Carolina.
July 12–17	Twenty-three people die, 725 are injured in riots in Newark, New Jersey.
July 23–30	Forty-three die, 324 are injured in the Detroit riots, the worst of the century.

1967 (*continued*)

July 26   Black leaders Martin Luther King, Jr., A. Philip Randolph, Roy Wilkins, and Whitney Young appeal for an end to the riots, "which have proved ineffective and damaging to the civil rights cause and the entire nation."

October 30   The Supreme Court upholds the contempt-of-court convictions of Dr. King and seven other black leaders who led 1963 marches in Birmingham. Dr. King and his aides enter jail to serve four-day sentences.

November 27   Dr. King announces the formation by SCLC of a Poor People's Campaign, with the aim of representing the problems of poor blacks and whites.

1968

February 12   Sanitation workers strike in Memphis, Tennessee.

March 28   Dr. King leads six thousand protesters on a march through downtown Memphis in support of striking sanitation workers. Disorders break out during which black youths loot stores. One sixteen-year-old is killed, fifty people are injured.

April 3   Dr. King's last speech, entitled "I've Been to the Mountain Top," is delivered at the Memphis Masonic Temple.

April 4   Dr. King is assassinated by a sniper as he stands talking on the balcony of his second-floor room at the Lorraine Motel in Memphis. He dies in St. Joseph's Hospital from a gunshot wound in the neck. James Earl Ray is later captured and convicted of the murder.

June 5   Presidential candidate Senator Robert Kennedy is shot in Los Angeles. He dies the next day.

1986

January 18   Following passage of Public Law 98-144, President Ronald Reagan signs proclamation declaring the third Monday in January of each year a public holiday in honor of the birthday of Martin Luther King, Jr.

SOURCES

The quotations in this book were selected from the speeches, sermons, and published works of Martin Luther King, Jr.

Strength to Love (Fortress Press, 1963).

Stride Toward Freedom: The Montgomery Story (New York: Harper & Brothers, 1958).

The Trumpet of Conscience (New York: Harper & Row, 1968).

Where Do We Go from Here: Chaos or Community? (New York: Harper & Row, 1967).

Why We Can't Wait (New York: Harper & Row, 1964).

"A Testament of Hope,"*Playboy,* December 9, 1968.

"Letter from Birmingham Jail," April 16, 1963.

"I Have a Dream," August 28, 1963.

Nobel Peace Prize acceptance speech, Nobel Foundation, 1964.

"The Casualties of the War in Vietnam," address at The National Institute, Los Angeles, February 25, 1967.

"I've Been to the Mountain Top," April 3, 1968.

The photographs incorporated in this book are from the following sources:

p. 2: Martin Luther King, Jr., courtesy Martin Luther King, Jr., Center for Nonviolent Social Change, Inc.

p. 14: Dr. King and Coretta Scott King on the march from Selma to Montgomery, Alabama, March 1965; by Steve Schapiro, courtesy Black Star.

p. 20: By Flip Schulke, courtesy Black Star.

p. 26: A fire hose batters blacks in Birmingham, Alabama, 1963; by Charles Moore, courtesy Black Star.

p. 32: By Dan Weiner.

p. 34: By Ivan Massar, courtesy Black Star.

p. 38: Registering to vote, 1964; by Charles Moore, courtesy Black Star.

p. 44: Demonstrating for jobs in Chicago; by Declan Haun, courtesy Black Star.

p. 48: Dr. King in the Montgomery, Alabama, city jail, September 1958; by Charles Moore, courtesy Black Star.

p. 56: Resurrection City, the Poor People's Campaign, Washington, D.C., spring 1968; by Robert Houston, courtesy Black Star.

p. 60: Dr. King in the pulpit of the Ebenezer Baptist Church, Atlanta, Georgia; by Flip Schulke, courtesy Black Star.

p. 68: The march from Selma to Montgomery, March 1965; by Bill Strode, courtesy Black Star.

p. 76: The March on Washington, August 28, 1963; by Flip Schulke, courtesy Black Star.

p. 80: Dr. King with son Dexter Scott, 1964; by Flip Schulke, courtesy Black Star.

p. 92: By James Hinton.

p. 96: The March on Washington, August 28, 1963; by Flip Schulke, courtesy Black Star.

About the Editor

CORETTA SCOTT KING is president of the Martin
Luther King, Jr., Center for Nonviolent Social Change
in Atlanta, Georgia — mandated for the purpose of
fostering positive social change through nonviolence.
Always closely involved with her husband's life-work,
she continues to devote herself to human and civil
rights causes, conducting workshops and lecturing all
over the world, inspiring others to keep her husband's
dream and philosophy alive. She is also the author of
My Life with Martin Luther King, Jr.

THE ACCLAIMED NEWMARKET *WORDS* SERIES

The Words of Martin Luther King, Jr. Calendar

Quotations from letters, speeches, and writings, illustrated with inspirational, historical photographs. Highlights important events in Dr. King's life, North American holidays and astronomical data. For all ages. 10 X 12. Shrinkwrapped.

The Words of Martin Luther King, Jr.

Selected and introduced by Coretta Scott King

Over 120 quotations and excerpts from the great civil rights leader's speeches, sermons, and writings on: The Community of Man, Racism, Civil Rights, Justice and Freedom, Faith and Religion, Nonviolence, and Peace. 16 photos; chronology; text of presidential proclamation of King holiday. 128 pages, 5⅜ X 8. ISBN 0-937858-28-5, $10.95, hardcover. ISBN 0-937858-79-X, $7.95, paperback.

The Words of Gandhi

Selected and introduced by Richard Attenborough

Over 150 selections from the letters, speeches, and writings collected in five sections—Daily Life, Cooperation, Nonviolence, Faith, and Peace.
21 photographs; glossary. 112 pages. 5⅜ X 8. ISBN 0-937858-14-5, $10.95 hardcover.

The Words of Harry S Truman

Selected and introduced by Robert J. Donovan

This entirely new volume of quotations from Truman's speeches and writings gives the essence of his views on politics, leadership, civil rights, war and peace, and on "giving 'em hell." 15 photos; chronology. 112 pages. 5⅜ X 8. ISBN 0-937858-48-X, $9.95 hardcover.

The Words of Albert Schweitzer

Selected and introduced by Norman Cousins

An inspiring collection focusing on: Knowledge and Discovery, Reverence for Life, Faith, The Life of the Soul, The Musician as Artist, and Civilization and Peace.
22 photos; chronology. 112 pages. 5⅜ X 8. ISBN 0-937858-41-2, $9.95 hardcover.

More Inspirational Biography
Gandhi: A Pictorial Biography

Text by Gerald Gold, Photo Selection and Afterword by Richard Attenborough.
The important personal, political and spiritual periods of Gandhi's life. "First Rate"–LA Times. 150 photos; bibliography; map; index. 192 pages. 7¼ X 9. ISBN 0-937858-20-X, $9.95 paperback.

Available at your local bookseller or from Newmarket Press, 18 East 48th Street, New York, New York 10017, (212) 832-3575. Please add $1.50 per book or calendar for postage and handling, plus $.75 for each additional item ordered. (New York residents, please add applicable state and local sales tax.) Please allow 4–6 weeks for delivery. Prices and availability are subject to change. For information on quantity order discounts, please contact the Newmarket Special Sales Department.